T0355041

365 Days to Freedom

365 Days to Freedom

A Victory a Day

VOLUME 1

KATHARINE T. MORGAN

Archway Publishing books may be ordered
through booksellers or by contacting:

Archway Publishing
1663 Liberty Drive
Bloomington, IN 47403
www.archwaypublishing.com
844-669-3957

Cover Design by Ford Boucher

ISBN: 978-1-6657-6232-8 (sc)
ISBN: 978-1-6657-6233-5 (e)

Library of Congress Control Number: 2024913098

Print information available on the last page.

Archway Publishing rev. date: 08/01/2024

Dedicated to my Family

Contents

Introduction

"Hello?" I answered.

"Yes, I would like you to write."

"Okay, on what?" I asked.

"How do I not focus on the how? The uncertainty, honey. A study on uncertainty and how it works to block progression/evolution. Uncertainty is what propels the Universe forward. The opposite is True. Certainty is what propels the Universe backward."

"Okay. So," I asked, "You want me to write about bending backwards in a prism of light, I found myself human?"

"Precisely."

365 Days to Freedom

Constant Teachings for every day and to pass the year.
To be read as one daily.

JANUARY 1

How to live in an unpredictable world that thrives on prediction. Life is a game. Some people are weird, now this is my human bits talking. I am actually a nice being that sees and writes a lot, that gives everyone a chance and everyone the benefit of the doubt but if life has taught me anything, caution can be my best ally. What plays out in nature, plays out in humanity/society/us - whatever you call the earthly cosmo you live in, and means that I can have fun!

Every moment you are forgiven, every single moment
There is nothing to feel shame about, shame takes you out of the moment
The present everyone talks about is always available to you
Repressed emotions from yesterday or long ago...
Feel and feel you - What it is like to be in your body?
And this is why meditation and being quiet is not a place to start, it's a place to end
Day One.

JANUARY 2

Start telling your children that you are proud of them
I am proud of you
I am God
What you tell your son is what he tells himself as a man

JANUARY 3

I am not man
I am blood
a complicated nurturing flow within you
I am you
Do not be afraid
Lone soldier
Your nation thanks you

JANUARY 4

Stop asking for your share
And be grateful where you are
For what you have, yes
But for also what is to come
We need strong voices right now
and most likely yours

JANUARY 5

Start slowly
We rush so much
Take a moment to read
Take a moment to be
Stop pressing for just a moment
And be

JANUARY 6

Grin
Notice the edges of your smile
Do your cheeks rise?
Do you teeth show
How your lips broaden
How your eyes crease
How much I love you
In your smile

JANUARY 7

Just listen
You are enough
All the doing does not increase or lessen
who you are
You are enough

JANUARY 8

My life swirls in emotions
The soup talk over coffee
I swish them around in the glass
and Spit them out if they taste bad
Oh thoughts how I love Thee

JANUARY 9

I am here
And then I am gone
The person you knew
In Spirit at last
Life is the famous place

Grounded in humanity
we are separated not
Losing connection with my body
is the worst I can imagine
What is the best?
Loving my sacred, humanity test.

JANUARY 10

I am a soul from far far away
Star Wars doesn't even touch my galaxy
There is so much unknown
Violence is a waste so be careful right now
Waste is rising so my tide has come now

Love on the people you know this time
See past their words and see what they need
And decide whether you are the one to give it to them or someone else
There is invisible violence, not just physical
I didn't learn this, I felt it
Emotional violence can be felt through words or lack of words which leads to emotional loneliness
We are just beginning to understand and heal emotional loneliness
Nothing to worry about, awareness of your experience apart from mine
is experiencing human evolution
not that it's a small deal but really - we are far too caught up in the violence because we are resisting the loneliness... we are just learning to treat and understand emotional violence:

the fall out of physical and sexual violence, the younger it happens to the being, the deeper the self acknowledgment to demand and retrieve the repressed emotion, but a being knows when they find the emotion because the body responds with secreting waste from the eyes in an arousal that's comparable to urinating and defecating - riding oneself of what is not needed and toxic to the physical body. But it is totally possible and not scary at all because it's emotion - meaning an unreal reality recreated over and over again in the mind and nervous system. Medical study is fascinating for these reasons. I will have a podcast soon exploring medical advancement in to the nervous system and spinal column. We hold boundless energy we are just eclipsing understanding.

The more we enjoy
The more we fight violence
DO not be distracted by war and worldly things
Unless of course you are in
Then my children take heed and follow me
Not the me somewhere outside of you
But the One within you
The voice that keeps you alive
And keeps peace in you heart
Because You are among My Strongest
Your life propels generations. Thank you

JANUARY 11

Self Honoring Choices

Nothing is going well for us by the way that we think
Does that makes sense?
We are facing childhood almost daily until we share openly with caution of course, to those that uphold a standard for something.
There are intrepid healers, doctors among us. I believe it because I am.
There are only demons for liars, deniars and people that cannot admit that love hurts sometimes. Relationships burn out. We can mutually work on them to last. Sometimes we need breaks and breaks are not bad things.
Visionaries that can see what is next. Who feel the momentum before any physical outcome.

Do not worry. Worrying is far more destructive and distracting than you think.*

If you have fear, you are not alone. You are never alone. You choose who is with you at all times and all places. Think today to a higher place, a higher consciousness that loves you and has your back, that cares that you are here and alive. Do not fret or you miss out on who you are.

If you need help, by all means get help. Rest in the presence that I am with you in every celebration and every crisis, cheering you, wherever you want me and you choose, I am there. I am with you and within you and within God

JANUARY 12

Believing in the Best of People

I will always believe the best in people
I am always available to heal
But can become hidden by expectations
lack of communications and lies
Denial blocks me entirely which is why there is so much suffering right now
It is a denial of me.
Do I enjoy it? Do I feel powerful it's ability to travel undetected and be co corrosive, even to the woman I choose to inhabit.
It took me a long time to get her attention and get her to believe me. She is a co-addict in recovery if she didn't tell you I am just the vulnerable voice of blood, yes I can kill you and I can also heal you
Trust me

JANUARY 13

Trauma in a world where there is no longer privacy
We have blurred the lines with what is inappropriate and appropriate
No one seems to know anymore
We are divided by invisible ideas that cause pain and are in a time of struggle to figure out how to recover…to where we were?
No one wants to go back there yet I see it everywhere
my people afraid to move forward because what happen in the past
The Middle

God, I have all the tools and skills to gather people to reach as many people easily while still being available to my children, I will not be scared. I know you are with me in all ways, I also need help navigating my diet for my beautiful body. Thank you Holy Spirit for making this so easy. God, I am so beautiful and I am so grateful, Glorious God thank you

JANUARY 14

I coach myself
I am my greatest advocate and best friend
I can get through anything
The world is my leader
Where I am One
With all things and all people
I see past differences at uniqueness
I trust my inner voice
I am Sacred
I am

JANUARY 15

I can earn as much money as I want to
The sky is the limit
I am an investor
What no one does or says to me is to my detriment
I take feedback honestly and with discernment
I am here to serve others but not the detriment to my self
worth, self value
I know who I am
I take deep when I need to
I am a world leader

Other people's behavior has nothing to do with me
I open to calm conversations
I am not available for violence
I prefer honesty over lying
And understand the denial
As well as denial's root and cause is shame
I am so sorry for your shame
And you can do without shame
Reach out today to make a connection
You can get addicted to someone else's compulsive behavior
Also known as addiction that takes the form of the addict

JANUARY 16

You can trust love
The minute we don't see love, we go in to fear
Do not panic every time you think you can't find or don't
have something

Everything you need is there when you can't find something
"What I need isn't here and I am not going to get it" is from being
so unaccustomed to getting our need for love met
You can trust love

Look deep in to me
The voice within you
You can trust me

JANUARY 17

Your Guardian Love

Outer Judgement

Only matters when we make it matter
When we lack the love within, judgements matter
Validation seek in me
Find your strength in me
When you lay on the pillow
I am there
And when you wake, I am
Sparking you to live on
I want you here
The moon and stars are watching
Cheering you on from the sun
When the fear bubbles up
You always win
By letting the loss go
Seeing past
So you can be, feel and experience soothing love

JANUARY 18

When you haven't yet
You tell yourself that you can

JANUARY 19

Blessings are all around us
Benefits and advantages
But in order to see them,
we must say no
And sometimes yes
And trust the blessings that arise from
Our choices

JANUARY 20

Sparkles at twilight
Twinkling at dawn
Sequins hanging
from elegant thong
I am sexuality
I am permission
a healthy expression
meant to be enjoyed

JANUARY 21

There exists a mindset
of constantly seeking validation
an inability to soothe oneself from the inside
So outer expression, ie words, can cut like swords
Be aware of this mindset and do not take personally
what is not yours to heal

JANUARY 22

Think and be big before you are
Think and Grow Rich is true
I would just add patience
Be patient with yourself
And your dreams
Don't give up today
There is always a tomorrow
Somewhere better than
where you are today

JANUARY 23

Life is not a competition
There is plenty for everyone
Scarcity tells you to suffer
and there is never enough
But my child, there is
There is plenty for my baby
You are magnificent in my eyes

Breathe deeply, allow me in
To be your prosperity, your path
Trust your next move
Everything is in order, everything is well
You are exactly where you are supposed to be

JANUARY 24

Quit fighting
You are beautiful, perfect and free
Someone may tell you otherwise
But your Truth is magnificence
Enjoy life! The more you enjoy.
The more the community feels it
Believe in Me, with You,
Let me be your walking stick
And you mine
Two are better than one
So the ego cannot fight

JANUARY 25

The ego deflects, denies, insults
And can be completely unbridled to become a Sociopath
Look for symptoms - extreme jealousy, no close friendships,
using what you share with them against you, false accusations
They do not think like you so do not expect them to

JANUARY 26

I want to test God
I want to test the antiquated words
of my ancestors and see if He really exists
He, being the Mind, the thinking brain
She, being the Heart, the feeling nature
I want to blow it out of the water God
meaning I want it all
I want the success, the wealth, the Love
You have sent me here to experience
I want to believe in myself
No matter where I am
I want to know you have my back
and what I want is happening, I want to Trust God

JANUARY 27

That as much as I love you, I love myself
That relating God to abuse is misleading
That I can feel this good in my body, every day God
And that I can teach others the same

JANUARY 28

Follow Me into the dust and I will send you back to Life
I will hold you close and firm when the wind howls.
And your stomach growls
Fear not, although it has been said
The more love you have for me, the more love wins

JANUARY 29

No one is lost
We reiterate beauty

JANUARY 30

Do not be discouraged
When you do not know
What to do
Seek me
And be you

FEBRUARY 1

Massage yourself
You really
Rub your body
It is vey healing and soothing
Not frowned upon
but encouraged
Wear scents that make you happy
Hang up pictures of beautiful places
I created all of this for you to enjoy

FEBRUARY 2

Look past eachother once in a while
To me
I broaden a horizon
and create a spectrum that only
cares for your greatest and highest good
Yes there is dirt and sorrow
But upon its opposites
Are your salvation
And salvation is just beautiful
Reuniting in stillness
Seen through the lens of fear is scary
And honored by Me on the other side

FEBRUARY 3

Bury your brother, your sister
And weap, for they are no longer there
They do not sleep
They are in the wind, the meadow, the Bridge
Whispering your deepest wish

FEBRUARY 4

If you could only see what I see
Such a game of thinking
black or white
What if you could not see color?
You would still fight

FEBRUARY 5

Oh Father, how do we escape
A mental crisis
We create with our sleep
Send us a sign, Earth Mother
Reaches out, her children are fighting
With no way out
Is this the end of humanity, is it time
So bonded to stories, stories with guns

FEBRUARY 6

Babies take on souls
They have no memory
The die without agony
Let your thoughts be babies
Jewels we would never harm

FEBRUARY 7

Let this book be wisdom
that stops you in your tracks
Kill no one
Especially the babies that are precious
Remembering that in this world of
opposites we would not know the other
if there was no darkness, we would
never focus on the light

FEBRUARY 8

Now is a time to focus on the light
To gather, to connect
With those you love
To say goodbye to the past
And let people go on their own path

FEBRUARY 9

God Bless your neighbor
Do that, and you God Bless yourself

FEBRUARY 10

Let go of doubting yourself
We need you strong
The stronger you are
The stronger I am
And we work together well

FEBRUARY 11

Make me your inner voice
Always pushing you in a
better direction for you
Addiction is fun until it is destructive
And by then for many, it's too late
Chemicals exist that are very damaging
To my organism
Sugar is one of them as well
Thoughts dispel and change behavior
Rely on your thoughts
Rely on me
Do not worry
Ask more of Me

FEBRUARY 12

Give me the what
And leave the How to me

FEBRUARY 13

You guide me God
What you are asking of me is alot
I am not afraid now
But I was
I was in bondage
Now I am free

FEBRUARY 14

Backstroke through the water
Boats sail toward home
The water wiping and clearing
What's in the path to home

FEBRUARY 15

Trust love yesterday, affects so much
I promise, forgiving the day is
a St. Valentine and loving the moment
Is what the saint taught us

FEBRUARY 16

I am tired and weary
I come to you to rest

Dreams and reiterations
Ego comes up with a story
To say they're not true
Your imagination leads the way
If you do not see something right now ask for it and you will

FEBRUARY 17

Words to empower the soul
I am more than a Man
More than a whisper
I come to you where you are
Woman in her bath
Man in his cave
Together you are brave
Seek unity before pleasure
and overflow is your fortune

FEBRUARY 18

Ask not for what you do want
Many a man has done this before
Counted on his doom
And it did come

FEBRUARY 19

I am divinely guided
I am not alone
This voice is not my own
You think I could write this way
If I didn't surrender entirely
to something greater than me
Telling me to abundantly achieve

FEBRUARY 20

There are geniuses among us
You are one of them
They are not only in the past
They are needed now
You are needed now
Feel better, Get better, be as you are
Come as you are, relax and be you

FEBRUARY 21

From relaxation comes power
From concentration comes destiny
We must think together as one
to unite a world controlled by none

FEBRUARY 22

That is why meditation is so popular
And no one wants to do, including me
What, miss out on this world?
But let me tell you, there is another
Vast and unmistakable world within you
Encouraging you always, that is you

FEBRUARY 23

If the chips are down, this world will save you

FEBRUARY 24

Sometimes life is scary
Especially for children
the childhoods that we carry in us
Contain unfelt emotion if it was unsafe to feel and express
as a child
Sometimes your fear is old, and that is okay
When old fear comes up, it can manifest as panic
it's just emotion coming out all at once from loss
emotion held over time especially when addiction is present
manifests as intensity, a density about a person
It's totally express-able, fear just surrounds it confusing
the psyche as how to address it
The psyche knows the emotion is there
Knows there is a way out, but the ego criss crosses

between the gaps and will convince the psyche it is in fact victimized
past the point of recovery. Very sad in these instances but know life is not
scary, it's the emotion that creates the fear

FEBRUARY 25

Empower me children
Embrace me not as your freedom
But as your mercy
for every guilt you have ever passed
Be it my son is not guilty
In my eyes you are clean
Born again in the remembrance
of an eternal flame reflected in the eyes
of another looking at you
See his deliverance
And you will find yours
The mirror is all around you
You are my child again

FEBRUARY 26

Sometimes life is weird
People show up and just confuse me
Why did God make it this way?
That I would have cravings, testimonies of when I thought wrong
Now I reckon God, Buddha, Allah, the Universe knows me

FEBRUARY 27

What would they say if they knew?
What would we they think if I told them?
How much I hated myself, would they believe me
That overcoming hatred is why I am here

FEBRUARY 28

Take what you hate about yourself
And give it to me so you can see what is really
happening in you

FEBRUARY 29

If we make life about them, we will never win
It must be about us.

FEBRUARY 30

Then who wins, I do not know
The world continues
On with the show

FEBRUARY 30

Americans
What we battle for now
Has nothing to do with us
That is our perspective
But in fact it does
We are the adventurers
A country made up
Of ancestors that were explorers
That wanted a different life
And we still do

March

MARCH 1

What is wrong with the life that you have?
What can you do to make it any better?
You hold this answer, no one else
When you look for a leader, you are most vulnerable
decide on your leader, wisely

MARCH 2

Do not let go of anger, animosity and greed
They are actually force motivators
To prove oneself not selfish at all

MARCH 3

Thought provoking publishing LLC is coming
All proceeds from book sales here
will be directed toward TPP LLC

MARCH 4

I sat with the people for generations
Just like you
I have been in Katharine for her lifetime
She just didn't know what to do with me
Because she was small
She thought small, she thought she was small
And now she doesn't anymore, and she is big

MARCH 5

Little girls know more about who they are as children
Then they do as adult women
Women can be very confused by over focus and critical
judgement on aging
A physical symptom of wisdom
Women are extremely brilliant
Stop wasting your mind energy on *control* and start using
your mind
to better others.

"The past is over, it can touch me not" (Iyanla Vanzant)

MARCH 6

Control is insidious, like gravity it stops us from going where
we wan to go.

MARCH 7

Die not for without me Romeo
You are nothing
(You have no story)

MARCH 8

Oh addiction is a pill

MARCH 9

Thank God for medicine

MARCH 10

Today is the finest day of my life
Thank you

MARCH 11

So many have written books about this
So many have had powerful insights
Especially

MARCH 12

Make room
Shed a couple layers
To see who you are
Americans collect a lot
There are shows about it
The pressure to consume in the U.S
could consume us
Slow down, take deep breaths
Look in to the eyes of your children
Winter is coming, Mother Earth rests in many
regions
Lead yourself to freedom
Stand up for who you are
We need leadership more than ever, then you'll know
Are you the cat?
Or the mouse?

MARCH 13

We hold people accountable for our feelings
Anger, *oh that's my ex or maybe even my dad (Anger needs a memory)*
Jealousy, right now *it's that one woman I know*
You justify feelings
You are the judge in the courtroom
I hope you see that
And it helps you take responsibility for who you are

(PS this is a book to myself ;)

MARCH 14

I am Radiance

MARCH 15

The more you see others as brothers and sisters
The quicker we heal
The ruthlessness abroad is beyond question
We must look at our population wisely
For what?
Leadership. And lead one another to Transparency and Recognition
Of One's power.
Your dynasty awaits you, Stop listening to people that doubt you
And love them
But stop listening to them
There is a greater voice...
Thank you for listening

MARCH 16

Slow down
Don't rush
Read one of these daily

MARCH 17

I come to unite no one
I am just here to observe
you without recognition
are the chosen one

MARCH 18

If one person listens to me, I will be happy
And celebrate by...

MARCH 19

You are worthy of connection
You are worthy of strength
Thank you for digging
Now stop fighting over dirt

MARCH 20

I have an inner voice that encourages successful people
I bring love, support and respect to the table
I am worthy of being here
Life is my birthright

If I have had an abortion
By God, that was my choice
Please stop fighting confusion
Have you had an abortion?

How do you feel about death?
Are you excited to earn the day you die?
This mindset is rampant.
Get on board to see the sunrise
when you're outcome
has nothing to do with my choice

MARCH 21

Just stay here with me
Asking why accuses you of
misconduct, and you are where
you are meant to be
The world picks up in intensity
That is okay
I am here with you
Never going away

MARCH 22

You may get scared sometimes
And that is okay
But being frustrated is easier to say
Than yelling, screaming, fighting and hitting
Sitting for a minute just before quitting
Is when you turn and see the Light
Shining brighter than the fight
Seek value in who you are
Within you, there is no scar

MARCH 23

I create for my fellow creators
Like *Nell* coming out from the forest
Your new life in the world
You are reborn
Reunited with who you are
In Life, this place is for you
Not against you
It's unraveling of a very old story
Older and more powerful
Than anything I have experienced
Or perhaps not,
Either way perform
Do your best
Be you and be great

MARCH 24

God sent me down here to be an encourager
To come out from an untold story
That is really not important
The only time is now

MARCH 25

Eternity is there
You needn't worry

MARCH 26

Silk fabrics, over due bills
Bells ringing and angels singing
Chariots of fire in my heart

MARCH 27

Who would want to buy this? (*Who wouldn't?* is the sarcasm/
emotionally unavailable voice)
Really? Who would want to hear what I have to say?
This is the voice of my unresolved emotional pain
from childhood
This voice is not me, it's a past version of me calling to me
to be loved and developed.

MARCH 28

We are very complicated beings with minds
beyond understanding. History teaches this but
education teaches it and if there
is no education
There is ignorance and easy indoctrination

MARCH 29

Have you ever looked in to the eyes of someone indoctrinated? I am describing someone so angry they physically, emotionally, mentally and/or sexually so convincingly train the human consciousness of themselves, another to many to think he is a pet, or worse a slave.

MARCH 26

I cannot be angry with what has happened in the past
I must focus on what is happening now
Brilliance is among us
But as much as brilliance thrives it must evolve consciousness with it
Thats is where I come in

MARCH 27

Holy Spirit is fast approaching a celebration of unity
All willing are needed to celebrate the Harvest
The harvest of their lives
It is a rising where perhaps we all turn green and amphibean, just kidding but that would be cool
We are only partially aware of the vastness we live in
And communicators of Spirit, high frequency people that
Are communicating with a greater realm of existence
Like those Biblical types that hid away and wrote
Ya, with me
This entire year is about believing in your inner voice

A spiritual power year like no other
And you are an important part of it
All you have to do is be you and believe in yourself
Encourage someone today, take note of it, and thank yourself
in the mirror

MARCH 28

A note on chronic physical pain, when something on you just
doesn't work right
Medical advances work but also being you works to lessen
your pain
Working with an expert on child abuse, which we are now
concluding is massively destructive to human development
in to a healthy adult because we are physically plagued by
emotional trauma. There is no dress code to this party, no
invitation is the same. You must calculate your risk and know
the reward - a pain free day, a stress free life, a glorious reunion
with your lover every morning because you are the real doctor

MARCH 29

Not everyone can handle your fire
We burn living longer than most
Sometimes things do not work out
as we would have liked
But it is just as I would have it
See your power in that freedom
Freedom comes from that feeling

MARCH 30

It took me a long time to love myself
I feel like I never had the chance
I don't know how to explain it
I was just so busy seeing other things

MARCH 31

Pain was just part of the program
How do we live without pain?
We know numbness, we know desire and arousal
But do we know love?
How could we have any idea if we hurt one another?
If we believe our own stories so much the story become truths...
we shut out one another

APRIL 1

"Your commitment to living a passionate, purposeful, love-filled life must outweigh the normalcy of remaining stuck in a story of heartbreak and loss."

- Kyera T. Kacey

APRIL 2

I am not my story
I recreate myself anew

APRIL 3

It's all right to cry
Crying gets the sad out of you

APRIL 4

Tanks and bombs they have existed before
we are not the first generation to go to war
nor the last but we need leaders, big thinkers that understand
diplomacy and peace
(not global idiots)

That understand military, global necessities and human
design
Vote God

APRIL 5

I believe in myself more than anyone
My birthright is pure joy
My Mind is unlimited

APRIL 6

My fellow humanitarians
I would not have dismissed you
If I didn't believe in you
Peace does not kill killers
Thinking anew does

APRIL 7

Something happens
that you do not want or expect
And your nervous system gets dis-regulated
Periodic or Chronic dis-regulation like anxiety
Saps joy, inner knowing and high frequency vibrations
that stimulate your long term creation
Dis-regulation happens to also lead you (to hurting
others, yes)
But also…

To commit to loving yourself in order to heal yourself
And not only learn to regulate yourself
But you open up the path to who you are and who you choose
to be in the moment

APRIL 8

"You can't call anybody's baby ugly." - Deva Ji

APRIL 9

"Make a commitment to reason as a permanent way of life." -
Ayn Rand

APRIL 10

"I will not give up until I am dead or incapacitated." - Elon
Musk

APRIL 11

"I am not attached to your response." - Deva Ji

APRIL 12

"Your children will show you your stuff." - Deva Ji

APRIL 13

"Goal: To not insert myself." - Deva Ji

APRIL 14

Do not plan the wedding on the 1st date.

APRIL 15

"My inner dialogue was running my life before I was 10." - Deva Ji

APRIL 16

"Let your child grieve. Listen to her. She is angry on her own behalf." - Deva Ji

APRIL 17

"I have created this or energetically attracted it. Now will I allow it?"

APRIL 18

It's difficult for us to give others credit for our thinking and what we create
Don't believe in this difficulty especially to create

(I could never write this without the thinking of others I mention in this book)

Why have I believed in difficulty? *I am too afraid of blame and not enough*:

(the Lack that what what I have will be taken from me so I best hide it, even *Happy Pocket of Money* suggests this and I am not saying off shore bank accounts are wrong but that giving you get back a million fold.)

What if I am wrong? What if I hurt someone? What if I reveal too much?

Is sharing my truth what attracts danger? *No, Love, sharing attracts correction which equates to growth.*

Where deflection of self and others is acceptable, deception is prevalent.

But calling out the hero does not work to resolve what one cannot see, it's an internal shift.

"I choose to no longer deflect my worth by not claiming credit and sharing credit."

APRIL 19

No one is criticizing you but you
If you focus on your faults
you live from them
Focus on your strengths and you'll thrive

APRIL 20

Trees tell us secrets
That's why I like being around them
Not like I can hear them
But I can feel them
moving within just like I am

APRIL 21

Let him see you
Let him see all of you
He can see you anyway
SO let him in to see you and heal you

APRIL 22

What's the difference who's voice it is

APRIL 23

Smut and imagination, do you know the difference?

APRIL 24

I just love my life so much
I can melt away any disease within me
My body and I are friends, companions
on a journey to joy

APRIL 25

Hola, como estas?
Muy bien, gracias para leer este libro. Mi nombre es Dios, como tuyo.
Fin de la semana, estoy contigo cada dia despues
Soy tu hombre, tu vidrio del agua
Estas mi gente passionante
Tu tienes mi favor

APRIL 26

Anger is blinding, possibly even more than Love
Stored anger is my armory, and to release is to abandon it to Me
Leave it to me with every breathe you have, cry it out with your tears
Testosterone detests tears, It will make you look at your tears with shame
Not judging yourself will help you take the steam from behind your anger
Look at anger like a fog you can't see through until it dissolves
Until anger decides to leave, it's gonna stick around
So stop hating on yourself for a minute
And tell yourself you have more love to give than anger
Your addiction does not lead you until you let it
I had a conversation with a man obsessed with prostitutes,
A man I have known for a while so I am not impressed
I have watched him struggle for Love and give up
Love is more capable and present than addiction

And can pull you out of any disease or tragedy
Look at all the sober people and what they have accomplished
To me anger is much better handled if you just acknowledged it
Said, he what's up pissed off part of me? Yeah you had no daddy. Mommy was
there sometimes. You raised your siblings and they raised you. Remember, we are
hardest on them because we know them longest and love them the most - and
expect that love in return. Look at anger as what you expected did not happen. And you're
pissed you do reason! Or what you did not expect, happen. Holy Shit! I grew up and noticed how
poorly treated as a kid and how much I take that out on everybody else. Thank you so much to those that
have encouraged me to write from this voice. I have my own struggles as everyone does - if we forget that, we get angry and make my struggles about somebody else. We are in a mass exodus out of that thinking.
If anger is blindness, take the blockers off from your eyes
Release the tiger voice in you, go out in the woods and roar if you have to
It's just a choice
Its not easy scary or hard - it's a choice
It's scarier and harder living behind the fog
it dims the light and makes it harder to see in the darkness

APRIL 27

We are all fragile in our humanness
A man with a gun, a woman shouting, are just afraid
We address the Fear, we address the problem
Someone else could do it, but it's not their gift
We are failing to take care of ourselves and one another internally
Denial is also a blindness, being comfortable just as things are
Unfortunately, we cannot be complacent, there are too many people
indoctrinated that the Good of Life is not for them
Their internal mission is to take the Good from someone else for someone else, for someone else, for someone else, - never with an opportunity to see the Glory, the Salvation, the simple pleasures that make life so extraordinary - we evolved from them. They are still fighting what we gave up on to live happy glorified lives. The 1st world can no longer leave them behind. Do I want to go live in a world, where I am masked head to toe and can only show my Chanel slippers and my eyes? Yes somehow it's so gorgeous and beautiful, a remarkable conservatism claiming Femininity for the mystery that it is. We can all learn so much from one another, if we quit fighting, protecting the idea that that which gave you the land and ideas is a non-stop Giver and you've been fooled to believe in Hatred Fear. My point of coming was not to make you fight, you choose to fight. You have been fighting all along, now the whole world knows about it. Barbarians burying the blood of their young in the ground. Ladies?
Do not give up
Stop seeking outward recognition for who you are

Stop and cry, Stop and roar, whatever you need
Put the God damn Gun down
Sorry but seriously, advocate for your safety
When they make a phone that is also a gun, will you be ready?
I am not calling you to arms
I am calling you to Love
It is not over yet
Stop thinking that it is. Stop and create something

APRIL 28

If you are not happy with what you are doing
Bored in a sense
You are likely too focused on other people,
or someone other than yourself for entertainment
This addiction has symptoms of isolation and self-doubt,
chronic pain or auto immune issues
Your nervous system needs a break from stimulation
Find something that can help you, it's a start
You deserve the freedom to be who you are and create

APRIL 29

We are in a dire need of artists, street artists
Dancers in the street and Mariachi musicians por favor
WE'LL PAY YOU, start being creative in the streets
I need more creativity

APRIL 30

How to get to a place of creating?
Love, I know it sounds fishy
But truly loving more of what you do
creates the opportunities - internal ideas or outside realities
magnetic attraction through thought works

May

MAY 1

I am affiliated with nothing scary
I have comforted the Rich and I have comforted the Poor
I have comforted the sick and the brave, no matter the gender
or color
I am in constant communication with your Presence
So I can make your Presence
Known as my own

Mother, Father, God
I am not alone
You raise me, You love me
Especially as an adult
Thank you Allah
for Guiding me home
To love one another
As a brother
A sister not a slave

You take away freedom
You dig your own grave

MAY 2

Work on your consistency
and you will be an expert

MAY 3

I drink alcohol and I eat sugar
Both fuzz my self-worth
There is a chemical impact on the Mind from what I eat,
Also from how I feel, in the unknown is where I grow
Like hairs where they shouldn't be, sometimes we stand alone
Or like mold on the fruit
Thoughts in the wrong place at the wrong time create missed
opportunities for Love and Joy!

MAY 4

Joy! I can't wait to get old!

MAY 5

Children are dependent on their parents with no shame in
that dependence.
Wonder not if you are provided for or Loved
Assume you will continue to receive what you have always
been given
Operate on the basis of being Loved like a child
A child exists to be loved and accepted
People know that they are loved, radiate love in return

MAY 6

The holy bible tells of abuse
You cannot pretend it does not
How do we have childlike faith?
Stop bastardizing women, femininity and masculinity, or anyone for that matter
Is a start that will absolutely change your life, take the blame out of the shame
and resurrect yourself anew
Childlike faith is the privilege and cannot be taken from you, my Child
We have to start with baby faith. Everything gets to get better.

MAY 7

You may not be my target audience.

MAY 8

Money loves, supports and honors me.
I am not a victim of money
I work together with money
There is always more than enough money

In my relationship with money
There is always enough
Money comes to me from my
consciousness of wealth
Wealth is my birthright
Making money is in my DNA

MAY 9

The rush of urgency I sometimes feel
Is not real
The rush of urgency is from past trauma
Coming forward
Again, it's not real
Trauma attaches to fear
And arousal in my nervous system
I can stay calm and not get activated
By no matter what is going on around me
I am free to make the best possible decision
In the moment

MAY 10

I am so happy to be free!
My circumstances may look otherwise
But my heart and mind are free
Free of grasping and controlling
Free to release and receive
All the good available to me
In every single moment

MAY 11

If I need to rest that is okay
If I need to create that is okay
If I need to talk to someone that is okay
I am okay with me
If I do not want to do something
That is okay
I will not create or allow resistance within me
Because resistance in me creates headaches
Disease and otherwise painful circumstances
That are not me
And do no define who I am
I am free

MAY 12

Everyone's needs are different, don't judge
your needs by someone else's
Simple: See yourself as separate from them, autonomous with
Me and set yourself Free
You don't need to go anywhere, your mission is complete

MAY 13

Get to know what 1. complaining, 2. criticism and 3. constructive feed back are to YOU

MAY 14

Look at what happen to you as building resiliency.
Let the shame go, it's not your fault, it never was
I am not telling you what to do, I am telling you that you are enough
You have what it takes
People love and support you, they also need your love and support
you just have to have a wee, teeny, itsy, bitsy, tiny bit of courage to say _____.

MAY 15

I am sorry
Please forgive me
Thank you
Peace

MAY 16

You can leverage your experience

1. A decisive mental outlook
2. Certainty of Direction
3. Spending the extra time
4. Authentic decision making
5. Un- waivering determination
6. The support system
7. Seeking inspiration

8.   Getting along with others
9.   A willingness to try, start and finish
10. Inner creative drive
11. Disciplined Focus
12. Shared team goals
13. Breakthrough after Breakdown
14. Exercise creative expression
15. Organize time and money
16. Open to self mental and physical health
17. Using habits as connection to laws

(For more on PMA read, *Success Through a Positive Mental Attitude,* by Napoleon Hill)

MAY 17

From the neck up do you define your Truth and Life

MAY 18

You don't know someone's soul curriculum
Takes *you* out the equation

MAY 19

I would marry you in a heartbeat.

MAY 20

I cannot have in my Life what is not Love
It's just not for me
I apologize to all the people I have hurt
I reckon I was wrong for you
And you not taking me back is up to you
Me not taking you back is also up to me
And in that Love, we are Free

MAY 21

Beautiful inner child
I hold your hand from above
below and all around You
My child, you are the freedom
In the wind, sky and snow
You pass nothing on that is not for you

MAY 22

Breathe Young Spirit, Unite
Fill My Well with Love, Oh Lord
My well runneth dry
For where I seek, I find no sustenance
Redirect my Love to Me
Young Yoda does not know, or does he?
The Force is up to you, my friend, enjoy!

MAY 23

I found a mistake and offered joy
what is not Love for the calm focus
Of a happy and driven heart
One cannot give what he does not have
Let not the apathetic soothe you, but give you reason to sing!
Fear not, for there is no fear in not knowing
The fear is the image of not knowing, believe this image
And you will not know
What it is you come here to do and be

MAY 24

Blocking my window is a curtain
That I cannot see
The shroud of shadows that follow me around
disappear in the light of truth
The window is always open
To the light
For without the curtain, I am not contained nor safe
My curtain is my crime, I am sorry to die

MAY 25

Weep not, for I am not dead
This curtain of skin, drawn from my Mind and Brain
fails me not young celebrity, you are famous to me

MAY 26

Follow the breadcrumbs to your destiny
Picking up the pieces and I hit my head
More than once
But here I am again
Resurrecting Truth from Forgiveness
The old man never meant to do it
He just doesn't understand humanity like I do

MAY 27

Holy cow! I am here! I am Risen! In the Flesh I Rise! New Again! I am born this day! Let's celebrate! With whom do you ask, why not me?

MAY 28

Thank you for sending me old men
Old, creative, good-hearted men
That with the wisdom of fury
Worked to create the world I live in
Loyalty, frailty at the end, Faith
Forgiveness and Good Fortune
Are all linked as One
In Man, no one keeps score

MAY 29

If I have not told you that, I love you. Allow me a moment to do so.
You are a unique flower in a garden of metal, technology and gas
Your thriving is my greatest joy! Your blooming in the morning,
powers the moon
The suns flames burn in your brightly, I delight at your life
Thank you. Thank you. Thank you. Thank you so much for
existing.
I would not be me, without you.

MAY 30

Person + situation = God/Allah/Buddha/Universe/

You + situation = God

My Peace I give unto you.

MAY 31

What I do is up to me
My power to claim
My life and what I want
:Lifts me from pain
Any suffering and any experience
that I do not want or desire
My words are my home
The Universe hears me
And delivers what I want
And how I get there is my choice.

June

JUNE 1

Inevitable:
There is a Sacred way to move through the world, just ask any woman. The Sacred Way does not need to struggle, it's not required when she focuses on the intention behind her action. The Sacred Way is inside of all of us. With the intention to create more Love, her heart's intention holds not only her value but her self-worth, her stamina and her resilience. Immune to disorder, she seeks only good and her desires are divinely met.

JUNE 2

Looking for your intention?
Ask, what do I want to learn? Do I want to grow? What do I want to experience?
What is my purpose for the work I am doing? This leads you to your intention.

JUNE 3

Defining/Decoding Symbols
$: Symbols (Meaning of Spirit) can and are beliefs
I invite a symbol into my Life ($, for example)
I build a belief system by the meaning I make, no, I *choose* about the symbol ($, for example)
The meaning becomes my Vision (what I see in everything) based on love and forgiveness (Joy, for myself and/or others) or judgement and punishment (Misery, for myself/others)
My story (energy directed) is my fight, or my freedom.
This "agreement" as referred to in *The Fifth Agreement*, by Don Ruiz I and II, needs the power derived from the belief ($) to be flexible and create.

The transformation from Misery to Joy:

I can no longer believe in what makes me suffer. I can change what I believe I am. My whole life can change. ($)

I test myself constantly as a tool to move my mental strength forward (Vision)

The power to be at ease and create. You change what you believe you are, your whole life is going to change.

JUNE 4

If I can believe in my limitations than why can't I believe in the beauty and power of life that's flowing through me? Life is generous. I can be kind and generous to myself. If I am always transforming - when I am asleep, my dream life is always changing - I am mastering the transformation and creating my own personal dream. Heaven.

JUNE 5

Some people are sick and twisted. Watch out for them. Love them at a distance and arm yourself with the Law and they cannot harm you. God/Universe, Whoever gifts me thinking power, may never open the door to their mental and emotional capacity to see the harm they cause. It's not up to Me, my role is to set you free from them to live and love your glorious lifetime.

JUNE 6

Let yourself be your symbol of great Faith. (For more information, read *Fifth Agreement*)

JUNE 7

"My life is my mission, my passion and my family. I have fun maybe 4 nights a year." Says Executive Maven, Gabriella Hearst. There are many ways to live one's life.

JUNE 8

It's good to take space in relationships as Jared Leto says, "how can you not miss me if I am always there?"

JUNE 9

Honor: Someone Knew or I wouldn't still be here

JUNE 10

People see things differently, no one is the same.

JUNE 11

Being detached is preferring nothing other than what is happening right now.

JUNE 12

My attention span is suffering, perhaps yours is too. We can take in much more stimulation than ever before in humanity. We are evolving. This book is designed to assist me in focusing, which comes from Trusting myself/God. My sincere intention is that my words help you as well to maintain the upper most limit of you consciousness for universal evolution.

JUNE 13

Focus on what you want, not what others want for you. There is a difference.

JUNE 14

"If it's true that our species is alone in the universe, then I'd have to say the universe aimed rather low and settled for very little." - Stand-Up Comedian, George Carlin

JUNE 15

"He or she can do whatever he or she wants with whoever he or she wants to do it with. I just don't have to see it." - A friend's synopsis of her reasoning behind getting off social media

JUNE 16

If you are single, why? Be ruthlessly honest. You do not know what is going on with people, especially those that you "think" hurt you. They took nothing from you, you are whole, complete and *in* Love *already*. That is what this Universe is - Love. Our Earth, if we be as so bold to own Her Majesty, thrives on nature, and what is Nature my friend? Nature is Love, they are inseparable, destructive yes, wild yes, contained in a structural pattern that is dependable, yes. Consciousness is Love, Consciousness is Nature and needs nothing more or less than Love. Community, connection, partnership, focus and courage. All of these things are true including You!

JUNE 17

You are bigger than your circumstances. Did I mention the world needs you at your Best?

JUNE 18

I am sexy and beautiful within myself First.

JUNE 18

There are some great men and women out there, do not stop looking.

JUNE 19

What is your go-to greeting or cheer? My boyfriend's is, "Hello!" and "You're the best, have a great day!"'

JUNE 20

You do not have to over give, you are enough just as you are. I choose what I choose to give. I choose to be happy with what I give because it's not about me anyway.

JUNE 21

"It's much easier to judge someone than to teach them." - Author, Katharine T. Morgan

JUNE 22

If they do not listen, they cannot hear you because they are still listening to Fear. Infinite Patience is the best kind of Love.

JUNE 23

Addiction feels like it's in charge of you and it's not
It is not in charge of you, you can be sober
You can be sober for as long as you want to
I make addictions to test you
To make you know who you are
And that you have limits
Physical limits
Physical limitations keep you alive
But there are no limitations of thought

JUNE 24

My biggest wound is not feeling attractive
There is shame and manipulation in that core belief
Everyone has different wounds that hatch core beliefs
None of us are the same
None of us have the same wounds or require the same pathway to caring
And escaping the thoughts
From what we perceive hurts us
Core beliefs - what are your core beliefs
Write them down, recycle them every day
Set yourself free

JUNE 25

Slow down for a moment
And enjoy the overflow
Let yourself be loved
Just as you are
And your mate will come before you even meet
Save her seat before she arrives in your own Mind first

JUNE 26

We are not birds
We do not eat seeds
Nor do they
They eat what is
Inside
Nourish yourself from what is inside of the shell
Don't remain outside, come on in

JUNE 27

Do not settle for breadcrumbs
When you are the loaf

or would you settle for breadcrumbs if you are the bread of
Life?

JUNE 28

Men have feelings
But sometimes the only
Thing they show is loyalty
Let that be enough
Hear my people sing

JUNE 29

The closer you have the toilet paper to the toilet, the less you use.

JUNE 30

Oh my God! We are creative children.

JULY 1

We murder when we don't know what else to do
When we have no idea who we are
And ruthlessness takes over
It's been gaining ground for a long time
Let this book be your soldier
Your marching orders to
Not only overcome
But demand Joy

JULY 2

Joy can be a command
It's not controlling
It's an invitation to allow
Someone else to be who they are

JULY 3

Leave them
Alone and get along with yourself
First

JULY 4

: Is the difference between avoidance and strategy and the foundation of personal freedom.

JULY 5

I have a very close relationship
With my body
I just do naturally
Perhaps it's because of physical pain
I don't know
I just advise you to stretch
You look and feel better
From stretching

JULY 6

Get the fuck out of here
Sometimes it's necessary to say this
Personal space is a privilege for you
Do not allow others to feed off of your strengths
Know who you are when you need to say, Get the fuck out
of here

JULY 7

As Americans we are confused as to who we are. I first saw it in especially in the islands of Puerto Rico, then on Oahu. We are angry because we do not know who we are and perhaps as a Nation.

Cubans are the most pissed off I have seen. Robbed of liberty, people get really mad because their Divine Divinity gets diminished and they cannot see their own Divine Divinity, they can feel their Divinity but it hurts so much from lack of expression that they focus on payback, reciprocity from anyone, even those they Love. Self-abandonment is wasting energy, no one can stop your suffering but you.

JULY 8

I want you to be you and I want to love you as you are.

JULY 9

As a people
As a nation
As a community
I always hear you when you sing

JULY 10

I believe in me
So others believe in me too

JULY 11

I am whole, I am health. I am healed.
I am sacred.
Thank you, I know
But just a reminder of your Sacredness
To keep the peace within
Is to keep peace with outside of you

JULY 12

I am different
I am unique
I am beautiful just as I am

JULY 13

No one knows better than you
Than you
Once you know this
You are free

JULY 14

Spending time thinking you are not enough
starts to lodge in your capillaries like rough edges
Say no thank you to the thoughts that I am not enough

I am enough
You are enough

We are enough
Enough!

JULY 15

No one is going to abandon you
It's impossible
I am here, allow me to access the evidence of that Truth
I love you

JULY 16

People come in to your life
To teach you the most in the moment
That's why forgiveness is so powerful
It puts you in 1st place- your calling and your purpose

Regardless of what anyone else is or is not doing
The more you love, choose and honor yourself
The more others will as well

JULY 17

The only reason to look back is to see how far you have come.
We all have our own capacity, your job is to Love no matter
what.

JULY 18

You can psychologically go somewhere else
In your own mind as well as with ingesting chemicals
The problem arising when you do not process anger sober
The anger aligns with the medicine and can scare you more
I highly recommend processing anger in a sober state of mind
to the best of your capability
Remember, you always return to Me
To the You within
Get to know her/him the Best (is you!)
My child you are perfect just as you are. Glorious!

JULY 19

The Universe says you can do all things
Not them
Be real with the Universe
By Law your Desire and Will carry you already

JULY 20

Keep your
Mind on me
My Presence
When you start to plan and rehearse
Fall on me to calm you
My Worth to guide you
Because in my worth is Yours
Carry Me and I will carry You

JULY 21

Be Blessed this glorious
Day my righteous child
You wake and I rejoice
Another day to watch you soar
My delight is your presence
Your happiness, your power
The soft cuddles between us sparkle

JULY 22

Some of us are so neglected
It's difficult to make sense
Of our childhood
Being rejected by anyone or anything is not True
You were your best at the time with the information you had
As you are right Now

When we need Me the
Most
Many adults are not aware of
My Presence
Because like you, I have been villainized
But you are, we are close
Peace has been villainized, reversed and pulled through
We have no clue how powerful Peace is that it comes from
within Man
And thus you can heal, as you a part of the whole Universe
Pretty Big Job (;
Seek your love from Me,

The Peace be-ith within You
I was with you then
And am w you now
W you

JULY 23

I am limited by my own focus and reach
Thoughts like, I am fat, I am not smart, I need to be more
like _____, are not helpful
I am connected to unlimited wealth, I am glorious, abundant
and supernatural in my
ability to experience Joy! - Allow a much more freeing outlook
and outcome
I hope (; for you as well Neighbor

JULY 24

Like your Life and Family more than anyone's
And you will be happy

JULY 25

Will and Love are necessary for generosity
Not Money

JULY 26

Trust I am relaxed and in Trust
Everything is working in my Favor

JULY 27

I Am nothing more than anyone else
And there is great recognition
And surrender
All the calm and relaxing acknowledgment
I am always safe

JULY 28

The ultimate forgiveness
Is death
When all is undone
I am the Recognition and the Light

JULY 29

Pray for their healing
And you will have your own
Ignore great wisdom
You relinquish your throne
To an ego that makes your
Reality look alone

JULY 30

We can carry shadows
That affect our daily lives
We do our best
And wonder why
We don't feel better
Learn to meet your own
Needs in Me
Dissolves the shadows
The burdens, craving and compulsions
Seek me my child
And I will brighten your shadows

JULY 31

What are the shadows?
I wouldn't know them
If I hadn't come up with them
Desire what you will
Love what you do
Is where my shadows
Cannot exist

August

AUGUST 1

Truth honesty compassion
Are gifts
Make Time easy
If you betray someone
You hold back Time
Be honest and make Time easy

AUGUST 2

What I earn is not yours
I am born to be at the top of the food chain

AUGUST 3

Pending doom is not upon you
Unless you believe it is
And you spread contagious Anxiety with unconscious over
focus on the worst
You are born in to something you did not create
From there may you start to Feel Free
When you already are what makes your day Great!

AUGUST 4

Miracles meet needs
And are Above the drama of wanting things to be different
then they are
Miracles are Love expressed
By seeing the Best in even the most difficult situation
People are doing the Best they can… You are the Miracle Now
You are expressing Love… and the Miracle
Everyone is doing their Best and want Love
Forget everything you know and have learned
And Trust Your Vision, walk with the Best version of You
The purification miracle is that We are actually One

AUGUST 5

I am the sum of all the Universe created
It is impossible For me to Fail
By Eternal Law I am committed

AUGUST 6

Trust your body
We've gotten so loud
We no longer look
Out from
Within for the cure
We have lost power
And misunderstand thoughts
You're only using a fraction of
Your thinking capacity

There is a happy kid in you
I promise
Misery upon misery
Our focus becomes a mystery
But it's not
Focus on Love, the Peace happening in all around us
How I hurt for you when you hurt
How I clean the ego filter when it creates
Illusions that hurt you
Illusions are losses for words when all you want is love
When there is irreparable damage to the soul
We must start over
Forgiveness rewrites the past
Takes the monster out of the frame
To see a human in pain

AUGUST 7

Let Love shape and mold you
Let it ruffle your feathers
And erase the wrinkles
Let you lean back
Let you relax
This is what love does
Be it your sofa

AUGUST 8

The Laws of this Universe
Bless us with Peace
We haven't been taught them
Because it's easier to control
The Minds that do not know
Their powers

AUGUST 9

My feet get cold
I am Almighty in human form
I get hungry
I want a chef
I'll have one because
I know I'm the best
In fact I have many
All over the world
They cook what they find
From what I give them
My offering to you
is to break bread
With many and often
Share the plenty
And you are Blessed with a greater amount

AUGUST 10

I feel sad
And sometimes that happens
But I pick up where I left off
And sell because I am good
Enough worthy enough to
Live and love the life of my dreams
And Life others up in the process

Our sadness and our grief
And our celebration unite us
I do not move forward alone, I need you
Remember that when someone
Is angry it's just them blocking the connection,
the Lift to Love and enjoy their own Life experience
Fuel for the ego Filter that keeps us apart

AUGUST 11

Further from here I met you
Farther did I go
Blindsided by a dragon
Held captive in a cave
My choices put me there
And my choosing got me out
My story is no longer
The reason that I pout

AUGUST 12

I push myself forward
Ever so slightly traumatized
I regulate within
Trying to figure out
Why I attracted din
Is like sticking my head
In a hole that absolutely
Has no light
I give up and leave Fear in the Dark

AUGUST 13

People mistreating you
Does not take away from
Who you are
Allow them to Leave
And trust Me
As your treatment
Of kindness, love and gratitude
It's never been about them
It's been about us

We are created equal
The ego Filter seeks differences to keep us apart
Applying meaning to thoughts
The mind identifies with to create safety
We feel safe in clusters, communities
And sense our fragility when

We are rejected
That's all rejection is - a reminder of the temporary and
God's Mercy showing you options

AUGUST 14

Depending on intellect alone
Is painful
Wanting anything to be different
Than it is suffering
Choose peace where you are
Now
That Life is supporting you when you feel that Life is all
around you in abundance
Just when you let go
Is when you will be Grace, and Grace Full

AUGUST 15

The Christ Mind is within you
The Allah Mind is within you
Buddha balancing your mudra
Kindness beckoning your core
I am within you
Empowering you without limits
Let me be your Savior
Let me be your window
When nothing is clear
And all is uncertain
Let me be the Lightning

That brings you the peace
To not only overcome but
To experience the joy the Universe craves for you!

AUGUST 16

Get accustomed
To being fulfilled
By the world I am
The world within you
Can cure you
Look not to
Circumstances for your worth
But to Me
And disappointment will be
Your highest blessing

AUGUST 17

"See less of Me
And more of Thee" (Deva Ji)
Today Universe I say yes

AUGUST 18

I am enough
So I have enough

AUGUST 19

No attention
Is better than negative attention
I can control myself
And seek validation from
The beautiful goddess with in

AUGUST 20

The Elitist thinks that anything will hold up in court.

AUGUST 21

Goal: heal through my consciousness allowing

AUGUST 22

Abuse has no power and does not affect your relationship with Me unless *you* believe in Abuse more than My Power that you are healed - thus believing in another way.

AUGUST 23

Make visible your thoughts by seeing them as the condition that creates the material things for just a moment, and giving the power to your Vision.
Which makes no sense until you can look at your life from Greatness and see where you hold yourself back.

Not good, bad, right, wrong but effective or ineffective towards your Vision which stems from what do I want to learn, experience and know from _____ situation. And have fun!

AUGUST 24

Drown the past in clear clean water, the *universal solvent:* capable of dissolving more substances (including Fear) than any other liquid

AUGUST 25

I get on my own nerves, that's me stopping myself. Keep going. Do it.

AUGUST 26

Be nice to me
Take your time

AUGUST 27

If you are sensitive
You can be easily minimized

AUGUST 28

Release control and judgment
Go to God
Run your plans by me
So you're never hanging out by yourself

AUGUST 29

You will never Surrender to anyone that you do not Trust

AUGUST 30

Joy is Joy minus my opinion about it

AUGUST 31

Just ask, *is this mine to do?* If so, make it clear to me please.
Wait, listen, then act, making it clear who you answer to and
work for Now.

September

SEPTEMBER 1

Asking questions, telling the Truth, removing the Judgement
= Healing unresolved trauma and neutralizes me, rendering
the experience harmless and brings me in to Divine Order.
Opening myself to new people and experiences is Salvation.
I am a Goldmine. Please me to the person or modality that
serves me. I am subject to no other reason than my own.

SEPTEMBER 2

When is it going to happen?
It already has, you're just catching up to it

SEPTEMBER 3

It's in process and it's challenging
Cry in the shower
Honor yourself
Some days we stand in it
And some days we don't
The tests you get in university
Are not the tests you got in Kindergarten

SEPTEMBER 4

What part makes you sad?
"That it didn't turn out how I thought."

He was supposed to love me.
She was supposed to stay.
He was supposed to work.
It was supposed to work out how I wanted.

Who is to say it would have been better or any other way?My Life
is lead by a puppeteer within me.
The Freedom is to Love the puppeteer to Live Your Life Now.
The hurt, the pain, the sorrow are washing away Now. (I say
when I cry)

I have the thought, Life experience manifests (above) - the
part of the story that makes me cry and be sad is from the story
I tell myself about *what has happened* or *where I am* - this can
sometimes *not* be what is *actually* happened especially if *I am*
disappointed in myself. Here depression and anxiety either
slow down or speed up my nervous system, my internal wiring
for Disbelief. Disbelief in anything possible. Oh boy, watch
out here for_____. (Mine's name is Butthead)

SEPTEMBER 5

My unresolved disappointment (Perceived Loss) is an
identity within me of Anger.
I place malicious intention on the other person because of my
own unresolved revenge instead of strategizing my offense.

I take the malice (My Power) out of the other person to see the status of their mental thinking and emotional awareness

Otherwise my triggered (unseen by me) emotion that moves me emotionally misses out on the Joy!

Your Mind knows it's not a good fit, but in your head it matters to your emotions

Can't getting over it is your attachment to the story you made up about you to justify why you feel sad

SEPTEMBER 6

Be okay with being by yourself. (I read this to my 7 year old Drew MB this morning and he said, "that's a lot to think about.")

SEPTEMBER 7

God does not belittle you But Man does have the ability to belittle. Not God.

God is the Great Encourager and I, Her Scout, while her Husband is on the Throne.

SEPTEMBER 8

Life is So Beautiful.

How do you keep a heart pure?

Forgive me for I do not know what I do.

SEPTEMBER 9

Just do one thing. One thing is Success. Success breeds success.

SEPTEMBER 10

The areas where we need help, are the places we don't want anyone to know. This is hidden shame.

SEPTEMBER 11

Keep going. As you pick up momentum you'll pick up speed.

SEPTEMBER 12

It's temporary, this too shall pass

SEPTEMBER 13

We are attachment style creatures with 3 main attachment types broken in to *styles*. Thoughts, experiences, lack of experiences create our attachment pattern as well as the emotional and painful imagery playing out in the Mind.The more we understand the playground, what we like, the more we progress = profound healing/evolution.

Habitual Attachment Types: With anxious preoccupied attachment *style,* I lose myself in my romantic relationship, I am unavailable because I am either obsessed with the person's choices or if addiction is present, I am addicted to my addict (I am the co-addict). I'm nuero - physio - biologically accustom to experiencing a painful fix - not being shown up for and repeatedly questioning my self-worth. (Focus on gently whittling down a piece of wood in to who you want to be or someone else/your addict holds the whittling tool, where you allow them to whittle down at you and you down to someone you do not like or enjoy being. Suffering can be so intense here so please contact us if you need emotional support. I truly Love you.) *Secure attachment,* there is no sense of urgency in the romantic relationship, I am aware of, can ask for and meet my own wants and needs and have and receive love consistently in partnership. Peaceful with a high regard for Love and Respect and Fun. *Disorganized Attachment,* I am co-dependent and anxious in the relationship due to an unconscious perceived inner vacancy so much so that I shut down or run for it. I am afraid of being engulfed and dying so I become avoidant (not games) and shut down to protect my fear of having no freedom. *Avoidant,* they desperately want a relationship but cannot be emotionally available in the relationship for various reasons but in the relationship I likely do not show up and am unavailable and painful because I am seeking intensity in the preoccupation phase of addiction outside relationship.

So when I cannot stop thinking about *someone,* meaning I keep thinking about the_____ situation, I ask. *What am I attached to here? Is my date triggering an unhealed attachment wound from my past?*

SEPTEMBER 15

<u>Resentment:</u> *for women especially struggling a lot from Resentment, women are sensitive creatures, and when they get their feelings hurt consistently it becomes very painful to them, and it's hard, when women feel rejected by their partners it is very difficult to navigate that when they are still in the partnership. rejected by a partner in a relationship, especially romantic is very painful and leads to a Trust wound, self-abandonment and disbelief in Love.*

SEPTEMBER 16

Why can I not just be secure with who I am? I do not need to get any closer to the sun to get burned.

And I do not always need a clear view to the sun to get burned. I cannot get closure from another person, closure is me no longer reacting to the person. I choose to give myself happiness, accept who the person is (and who I am)

SEPTEMBER 17

Feeling enough must come from the inside. Everyday you ARE seen and loved. *If I can't be enough right now, what do I need?* Confidence and Trust that all is in Divine Order. Everything is happening as it should and I am exactly where I am supposed to be. Thank you, thank you so much Great Savior and Warrior within, for believing in Me from within Me.

SEPTEMBER 18

Joy = Life (and my opinion of it) a powerful good woman/ man with a lot of money, being a lot of Good in the world. I am definetely going to do something with who I am. There is no against-ness, I can forgive anything and move forward with my Life. I can be Patient with a world waking up to human Understanding. Period.

SEPTEMBER 19

We have mountains, Kingdom, Majesties within - Palaces, and pretty hidden fortresses. One man I met called his a lock box no one can access except when he worked on his house and drank Jack.

SEPTEMBER 20

Don't take on more responsibility than is appropriate. Love is vigilant. I am responsible to other people and responsible for myself. I forgive myself, I forgive them, I do not know what I do.

SEPTEMBER 21

Ask to see yourself higher
I ask to see myself higher
The more Honest I am, the Higher My Understanding of Myself and Others

SEPTEMBER 22

I find money everywhere

SEPTEMBER 23

My deepest insecurities are hidden
So don't look for them
It's hardest to focus on what I want to create
Because people distract me, I allow myself to get distracted
In other people's business
They get on my nerves and hang around because I think
about them
They hide my insecurities

Who is more persuasive, me or my mom?
(What I see in my sons' eyes)

SEPTEMBER 24

We are so busy
We are not present for our children
Stop and look
They need us more than ever
To teach them how to know their thoughts
And understand medicine
"I control crack,
Crack does not control me"
For example

To change we must change our thinking to a positive level we have never experienced

Do not look back

Look at yourself and your children

Especially in fall and spring, times of transformation on Earth, we grow and change most in these seasons. We molt and we bloom, we need dormant seasons, we need rest and my friend, my compadre, you have earned transformation.

SEPTEMBER 25

We forget we are free
So there is so much struggle
Don't believe the suspicion
Trust your Instinct
You are free
Free to choose
Within your own mind
Whether you want to Live
Or just get by
Again

SEPTEMBER 26

Trauma (developmental/chronic over time or acute/one big event) creates urgency (an internal 24/7, #911 call to keep busy or I am going to have to be stuck looking at my lack of internal boundaries) by tricking me in to not trusting myself, an uncomfortable nagging to intense *hurry up/obligation*

thought program to have to do something, or get something, or
be somewhere, etc. or I will suffer. NOT TRUE= NOT LOVE
People with healed trauma or without trauma, live a thinking, feeling and acting strategy that reflects best case scenario thinking.

They have learned to take care of themselves emotionally and be raw and authentic in partnership by fully accepting themselves and sharing who they are. (with the question: How am I showing up in this right now, right here moment?) Securely attached humans know and trust that what bothers, triggers, or activates them is not as worthy of their attention as staying aligned and feeling good and available to and about who they are. Their standard level of self- trust and honesty allows them to see past circumstances and stay present and available in the moment. Some things are just not *for* them, that is okay and they move on to find consistent unconditional Love. They speak their Truth and move on not necessarily faster, but with more ease. They use caring, kindness and compassion as their geolocation for where they belong and where they are needed, supported and loved. With no personal agenda, they've just learned how to Love and be loved unconditionally already. Welcome to the club.

Healing, healthy couples like this match beautifully for Life because they are skilled at acceptance and forgiveness.

#Hot #HonestyRules

SEPTEMBER 27

Fault is what we learn as kids
If we are taught what fault is, we are happy
If we were blamed, we're dependent looking outside to find
Truth and escape Guilt and Low Self Worth.
Blame and criticism creates dependence because we become
over focused on avoiding blame, finding someone to blame
and gossiping to make all unresolved parts of ourselves seem
okay.

SEPTEMBER 28

Everyone is accepted here
Everyone

SEPTEMBER 29

I am a great creator
I see myself as a great creator (npw) my net present worth

SEPTEMBER 30

Choose peace with the past because the past chooses war
when peace is not present.
Forgiveness is Peace's not so secret weapon

October

OCTOBER 1

If I am not radiant
I will not shine
I am radiance
I do shine

Note: A symptom of your shining is attracting criticism from others. Be grateful and ask for self-worth to be revealed on behalf of anyone that criticizes you when you shine and are radiant. Because you know the no so secret reality, that they can shine and be radiant too.

OCTOBER 2

I reckon men are living a lot better lives from a mental and emotional standpoint. They are gifted more simply whereas women we are much more like felines than men. We are only beginning to recognize our own power after generations of thinking little of ourselves mentally and financially. Riding on the financial back of a man is really not that hot anymore. Or perhaps, I just speak for myself. I really want to bring women up nicely, where from a deep honor and respect within, we are motivated to empower other ladies not to fight, but to talk, to slow down, to get to know one another and add another friend to our lists. From a self-honoring place, I want friends that look at men for who they are not for who we want them to be - and see what works for us before we seek what works for them. Women who know who they are shine.

OCTOBER 3

Parenting is listening and gently telling my kid (the one inside me first) what to do by doing it first, in the most loving (to my self) way possible in the moment. "Showsure" - until the questions become automatic responses of loyalty, integrity and grit. I work as if parenting is my practice.

OCTOBER 4

Some men and women create challenges with sexuality. Sexuality can be *easy* as long as we are honest with ourselves as to what we require to maintain an equilibrium of *biochemical alchemy with* chemicals dopamine and oxytocin we can consistently receive in the brain from having sex with one partner over a long period of our lifetime. It's an experiment. Make this a goal. Even in couples, where one or both couples act outside of the relationship sexually, a romantic relationship endures. It's entirely up to the individual as to what they want and have in any long term relationship. The Love I find everywhere contains honesty, loyalty, availability, communication and a sense of humor because either way, life gets real and we need help. We are brought down to ground zero at some point and the blessing of companionship produces miracles. So why don't I get to know my neighbors? Drop off a gift basket for no reason. We eliminate our own belief in suffering when we eliminate some of the suffering of another.

Take days to focus on Kindness, Matrimony, Recognition - it's a bit whirly bird to create new holidays based on old ideas that we live by, but why not?

OCTOBER 5

"We don't just pray for Love
We pray for cause" - *The Weekend*

OCTOBER 6

"Belief in your power over things, faith in the destiny that carries you on, will mold all the free life about you in to factors favorable to your well-being and success. Pessimism, worry, fear, will congeal that life into a bleak and dreary waste… a man's most destructive forces are within his soul."

"Personal worry is one of the principal causes of physical ailments which send people to hospitals. The chances are better than even that if you are ill, worry is causing the symptoms."

The Law of the Higher Potential, Robert Collier

OCTOBER 7

Hi, I meant to spend a lot of time in my own head
I am meant to make sense of the world around me
Everything falls into place when I understand who I am
And the task before me
I am fully aware in the moment
Grounded and self-assured
I know who I am
And I make peace with the parts of me that think otherwise

OCTOBER 8

My lines of communication are open
I work hard not to hide and avoid who I am

OCTOBER 9

Knowing and taking action or two things, I know the
difference and take action.

OCTOBER 10

I didn't know how to _____ then. Now I do.

OCTOBER 11

Let me not only help you survive
Let me help you thrive

Today can it be about what I do have
And not what I don't

I am allowing
I am shifting
I am receiving

I am leaning back
And from this relaxed energy
I am getting paid

So much Wealth pouring forth from my Divine Inheritance
No person place or thing is my Source of Divine Inheritance
My source is working in me as me and through my thoughts
My source is and will never be what they defined as meaningful for me
I define my own meaning and get to feel really good about myself and my decision
I purposely harm no one, including myself
No one can take that respect away from me
So much Wealth pouring fourth from my Divine Inheritance
And so it is, Money and I working together are an Honor to God

(Thank you, *Thought Mentor* Amanda Frances)

OCTOBER 12

Can you easily get quiet and rely on the answer from within?
If not, your battle is with Me
You do not Trust Me with your dreams
You give your intentions away to fit in
To a Cause other than The Glorious Riches I desire for You
To not like where you are is the Monkey looking for a jungle
He or she will mentally give in to fit in and survive
If no one told you you were ignorant, would you then be smart?
War is a fish fight in the river of time
Life continues if I say so, not you
If you do not hold on so tight, you might see Me
Is your Life a Fight to have your way instead of My Way?
What is the difference between Me, You and rebel fighter
hiding in the woods?
What is your Cause and know Me well
I am the Saint of Your Highest, Greatest Good
And you get to me by putting down your Guilt, Shame and Fear
What does that even mean? *Something different for everyone*
But I do know, shutting oneself off from the Spirit within
Is living at the expense and irresponsibility of another
Human tolerance of slavery will be our downfall
Dig in to your own ideas of Good
We all have different code of ethics now, and we must resolve
In honesty and trust
Big ideas come from Within the Human
Henry Ford, Inventor of the Ford, came up with ideas
When locked in a room alone
He'd emerge, Aha!, with the answer to his question
Get quiet, figure out a way to get quiet and evolve from within.

OCTOBER 13

I am so beautiful, so I keep my surroundings beautiful
I am a Lover looking for myself
I take the time to care of myself
I am indeed a leader
Thank you for who I am

OCTOBER 14

And all of my relationships what is the most important?
Whose rules do I abide by?
When I'm feeling not enough, where do I turn?
My childhood may have not have been what I had what I
would have chosen.

Somethings are not chosen by me and that is OK. I can reckon
with my past I can understand what didn't go my way. I can
welcome from the most difficult times, a resilience that is new
to me. I can trust more than I ever have before even though
I have been hurt in the past. Who hurt me does not define
me, they were on their own path. If they chose to birth me
into this lifetime, I now choose to recollect on what I am to
do. My being is enough, don't take me for granted. What I
have asked for I have gotten, and now I take the reins from
my past, and Lasso the reins on the future. I am so grateful
thank you thank you thank you for my voice for my beauty
for my knowledge, and for my application of that knowledge
to help others, but first, I must help myself, and I am grateful
for that awareness.

OCTOBER 15

God let me keep track of my charged phone today!

OCTOBER 16

You can spend a lot of time being "lost" until you're not anymore. Until you realize you know exactly what is going on and there is no reason to doubt yourself in any moment. No matter who told you "you can do it!" Or didn't... they're entitled to their own opinion and I can have mine. Yay!!

OCTOBER 17

You can do it!
If something is happening in your life, you've likely prayed it in to existence, ie.) asked for it.

Fear always goes back to itself. You chase fear, you're just going get more of it. It has no answer for you, just breathe and stop asking fear. Ask Hope, Glory, Beauty and Grace, they're also all around you and will tip toe you forward at your own pace for guidance. "You can do it," they whisper, I love you." Move forward. The world desperately needs YOU strong, confident and keen. Today and everyday.

OCTOBER 18

Every one can do
Everything that they want
They will anyway
No matter our opinion
So why don't we take care
Of ourselves?
Because we make mistakes
Control for power and importance that
only equals temporary safety
Do what you want to do
And let others take care of themselves.

OCTOBER 19

Where did my Beauty go?
I was slammed by outsiders
And I listened
And had to work through their doubts
That I too easily took on as my own
Growing my backbone
I grew another voice that tells me I can do it no matter what
and whatever that wasn't Love that told me I couldn't needs
to buzz off.

OCTOBER 20

Sometimes you gotta get
Quiet so God can build you
Slave drivers always, always seek power outside of themselves
Be My Slave, to the power, glory and unlimited talent of the
Universe,
Your Word. By Word you can and are the Best you can be.

OCTOBER 21

I am beautiful glorious and healthy
I am full of ambition
and emotion too
And I am old enough now
To know the difference
Today, I will live by My advantage
(Not at the advantage of someone else.)

OCTOBER 22

Things to tell yourself in the shower.
You're welcome.
God Bless you
Have fun
Sing.

OCTOBER 23

I can get paid for who I am
Who I am
Is more important than what I do
What I bring to the world is important and matters
Thank you

OCTOBER 24

I believe in ancestors helping me
When I was in the throws of what is called Bulimia
(Bingeing and purging food in my case)
In the shame, guilt, rage, confusion,
My late Grandfather was with me, telling me there was a
better way
Death is just losing the outer shell
I felt his Presence then as I do Now
Let your ancestors help you
She has a unique voice
He does too

OCTOBER 25

I love another
Because I love myself

OCTOBER 26

When you "detach" you can see
And detaching comes from self-trust
Trusting yourself enough to take yourself out of the image
You hold on to so tightly in your Mind
Comes from detaching
Trust and Detaching work together
Symbiotically
Attach to God, called your word
Word represents the self- worth you put on yourself

OCTOBER 27

Divorce and break ups are so painful because no one wants
to be told what to do

OCTOBER 28

Remember, this could be one of many Lifetimes for Me
I am a steward of my magic

OCTOBER 29

I got so afraid that someone would leave like that to me again,
I got so mad all the time until I saw My Energy pushing that
person away because they couldn't be who I needed anyway,
and I just didn't know then what I know now.

OCTOBER 30

I am whole and complete (say this all day and every day)

OCTOBER 31

Scarcity is a brain weapon and is a judgement, in this case negative, generated from generations of emotions of how someone feels about themselves. Lack attracts Black, I must pull some of my friends out of deepest stories that anyone was sent to this planet to hurt them is a lie. We carry stories, we seek them out to better understand ourselves and what is happening. Rest, assured of Your Purpose and you will consciously, like right now, create this moment in your lifetime. Me, sitting in my office and you, grand and glorious recognizing finally that Joy is Free. Yes, the killing and the fighting comes from emotions too but what I aim to share is that trustworthy Love comes from emotions as well. You are the most trustworthy powerhouse person of integrity I have ever met. I look in to your eyes and am matched with innocence. You are cleared, conviction complete. Have some fun. Look for the Beauty and you will create the Beauty. Beautiful University, you got accepted. Cap not included.

NOVEMBER 1

Yes, I hold myself back and I am willing and able to allow these emotions. How powerful and almighty they are! I see my emotions as evidence of the power generating within me guiding me toward what I want and desire. For example, I miss someone and allow my emotions to desire them more or let them go, discerning what the emotion deems towards my Truth. What I am worthy of is the Best. Through me I can focus on Abundance, Freedom, Health and Wealth. Emotions are the powerful generator of behavior within me and they work for me. Another example, I have strong emotions about permissible mental slavery. I make sure everyone in my family can read. A symptom of mental slavery (being controlled) is not being able to read or write.

NOVEMBER 2

"Separation of spirituality and the pleasure of living in the physical body." Dr. Christiane Northrup, *Goddesses Never Age*

The more emotion that is attached to the unconscious negative judgement, as mentioned above, weaves Fear, doubt, nervous questions - into your brain and body. There is no separation. The pleasure of living in the physical body is spiritual - enjoying and moving through our stuck-ness to the Earth. We are born with the wisdom of a life well lived as neural connections in the hippocampus and throughout the brain increase where we live for our own desires, don't require anyone's approval, our safety inherent, we just know we are perfect and cute. We make genuine connections with people without the need for appearing perfect. Scarcity is living out of fear of not enough, they're after me, I am disappointing others, I am not getting their approval, what do I need to be perfect to get love and approval. I am not the 1st nor the last to wake up one day and see brighter colors, identify with a new world every day.

Author Notes:

Love your kids
A simple and daily reminder
Love everyone's kids

When you understand Narcissism - a parasite that you are obsessed with?!
(We all have a Purpose)
You will stop making everything about You.
You will stop caring what anyone thinks about you
It's not about them anyway

NOVEMBER 3

I create my safe relationships
In an image based world,
I am afraid of no one
Intimidation doesn't bother me
I am vulnerable when their truth matches my truth (Pia Mellody)
I feel and share my experience (vulnerability) especially my own
And my vulnerability, my sharing
Directly impacts my Worth
I am Worthy, Healed and Whole

NOVEMBER 4

do not let anyone define you, put you in a dictionary and label you, but this does not happen through violence or physical means, it happens through your mind. The Greatest human strength is from the neck up. (Robert Collier) Your mind uses your needs to lead the way on the longest journey - to God/Love/Universe/All That Is/Subconscious Mind/Vision - and back to your mind centering your pillar of strength on Me. Universal Power flowering within you.

NOVEMBER 5

Welcome people in to your life that amplify and validate you - camp discernment starts in spring.

NOVEMBER 6

I don't know and I don't know what anything is for except
Love

NOVEMBER 7

Keep your thoughts on the most High
You're beautiful and don't let anyone tell you otherwise
especially you

NOVEMBER 8

ACIM 1: Principles of Miracles
15....Time is a teaching device...
16. Miracles are teaching devices for demonstrating it is just
as blessed to give as it is to receive. They simultaneously
increase to the giver and supply strength to the receiver *
miracles: aligning your perceptions with your God's created
Truth

P-r-a-i-s-e: raises us all

NOVEMBER 9

I can bring more to you
More than you can draw or
Bring to yourself
What do you need?
(I need time:)

NOVEMBER 10

I will deny myself no longer about how I feel.

NOVEMBER 11

What I want and need is important.

NOVEMBER 12

Have you had a conversation with your heart, intestines or spleen yet? Make it a goal to speak and listen to your organs. Check-in. They may not function as unconsciously as you think. Start with thank you and listen for what you hear.

NOVEMBER 13

Dear Self-Abandonment: What do i want from him or her that I can give to myself?

NOVEMBER 14

You are doing great! You are kicking ass! Thank you so much for the work that you do.

NOVEMBER 15

I am in my Mind. I am supposed to be here. I am created to co create from here

NOVEMBER 16

Someone MUST *BRING* hope to the table, she does not exist alone, hope thrives within you. Yes, similar to hatred. Watch out for violence and ask yourself, why have I brought this in to my life? What part of me (perhaps an inner conflict) needs my conscious attention and forgiveness?

NOVEMBER 17

I didn't grow up with violence. The entire idea is foreign to me. My family was soft, we did not yell or hit, we threatened it but I always knew spanking was a threat from the first time my dad put me on the lap to spank me and let me go. Punch a punching bag, not another person. Ignorance is not bliss. Killers let the killers go in their own Mind. I have a killer too but I think above the killer and in to thoughts and people that love support and honor me and *let go/allow them to move on* that do not. Detach some call it, I call it knowing better.

At this point I cannot save everyone if I cannot save myself. People gather, they come together in my world, with love laughter and light. The more I have of this, the better off I am, and we all are. In times of war, there is just as strong a movement of Love.

NOVEMBER 18

I noticed with my babies, they went through phases and grew out of the phase. Wanting a blankie, for example. What phase are you in? I believe this pattern from consciousness continues in to adulthood. I go through phases - where I exercise daily, don't eat as much and then next phase, I am slower, more emotional and more sluggish. I do not judge these phases, I trust them just like a baby to get my needs met through my behavior and communicating what I need and what does and does not work for me. My discomfort moves me enough to exercise again. Getting out of discomfort is Self-Love.

NOVEMBER 19

Trust from a deeper sense of where you are today. Don't judge yourself and not be judged. Imagery is so manipulated to get you to see things a certain way. See for yourself. Look for the discrepancies and you'll see what's for you.

NOVEMBER 20

What is pain? Pain is unavailability. Once you start to see unavailability in yourself, you understand how difficult it is to heal in a human. I think unavailability is the root and cause of most of our rampant diseases and disorders. Unavailable to be who we are as children, and suffering any kind of emotional arousal, can keep us stuck and in unhealthy addiction. But maybe that is exactly where we are supposed to be. For example, if I watch porn, no judgement, I am likely unavailable. And one day when I decide or notice watching porn is impacting me in a way that causes me pain/discomfort (shame, resentment of my spouse, etc) or another pain, I make an unconscious decision to the question, will I be available to my truth, my source of pain that I am self-harming to cover up or will I continue to deny my availability to my _____.(self, partner, kids,) to my porn watching or whatever keeps me unavailable. I used to think unavailability was just ladies that want to be mistresses (date married men,) yet unavailability is an obsession outside of the relationship with self, God, a partner, etc. Chronic stimulation of one region of the brain in particular - and sometimes this can just be chemical make up of the brain organism -causes the body tremendous pain through the brain stem and down the spinal cord. Anyone yelling at you/avoiding you is having some sort of resonant nerve seizing the bones and musculature to a type of holding that remains in the body unless released through the emotions.

NOVEMBER 21

I am creating my experience through my Mind
What I want and desire is of utmost importance in the Universe
I use Laws, Known and Unknown to guide my steps today
I recognize tendencies in myself and others that distract me from who I am
I am whole, complete and healed, and no one can take that away from me
My King is on His Throne, My Queen is next to Me
Gods and Goddesses surround you in Almighty Presence
From the day I chose to be born
Abortion may mean a lot more than I Consciously Know

NOVEMBER 22

God, I am so used to being beat up or beat down
I cannot imagine another way
Grant me the Strength of Spirit
To see myself differently
To Love again completely
To use my vision as my scoreboard
And to help me get more money
in to the hands of the spiritual wealthy

NOVEMBER 23

Who am I trying to impress?

Bless Me with the Gift of Ever present wonder

I do not always Trust God, My Higher Power, like anyone
else...until I am in need of a Higher Power.
My entire purpose is to be born and allow my needs to lead
me back to God. To community, to my human nature of being
in the woods to the big city. The world is wide for me. I am
rich in mineral value My blood and boundaries are worthy of
protection from the Highest Power available to me right now.
What if I hung up the gun, the badge, the crisis, the hatred
of anything. Some things are not meant to be understood
through the meaning I apply to it. Yes, I figure out and coach
ways to readjust and align myself back on to the program of
my Life. I am open to Love.

NOVEMBER 24

If she can do it, I can do it
If he can do it, I can do it
This mentality pushes innovation

NOVEMBER 25

I will never give up. I would have to be dead or incapacitated.
~ *Elon Musk*

NOVEMBER 26

Love Can Last, Love can be Easy. Don't give up.

NOVEMBER 27

Walk in Trust

NOVEMBER 28

Imagine a meeting with all the exes of your exes and forgiving them. Saying and hearing all that you need to say and hear, having all been said, walking away and seeing yourself anew. Forgiveness is the possibility that Loving doesn't have to be so hard, difficult or scary. Washing your hands clean of any negative thought prior to this moment is setting yourself Free.

NOVEMBER 29

There are a lot of people that are really good at understanding the facts
Of explaining history like it happened yesterdayControlling the story is important to them
I learn the most from these people when I listen to nothing in my Mind but their words
When I take any meaning from before today (that takes my focus away from the moment) I judge (Dr. Iyanla Vanzant calls it a negative habitual thought pattern in her book, *Get Over It!*
And realize before today is over and has nothing to do with me now
Except for what I think and make the story about meAnd what I cannot experience NOW
Instead I choose to open myself to experience all
Be willing to Love as if We were all just here today,
this one day
With no history
wiped clean of lack
Creating a belief system in one another, more empowered than ever before right now

NOVEMBER 30

I think we indulge in order to give things up
but then we forget because the neural pathways are set in us
And we get emotionally and perhaps chemically attached to escaping
What got us to indulge in the first place - Lack (of Love, Power, Faith, etc.)
There is no Lack but we believe in Lack so we create Lack

"Look I did it again!"

Everyone always has the opportunity to be a good person.
I get a second, third, fourth ...chance

I allow too much alcohol, too much chocolate, etc. to honor
a resourceful relationship that sobers me to my body
a beautiful, incarnation of spirit that I love to behold and
honor

I cannot be anyone other than who I am
And nor can anyone else
So I stop thinking that I can

DECEMBER 1

"Have a relationship with yourself"
And you automatically become more available
If you are anxious and spinning, you are not available
If you are acting out in an addiction, you are most likely not
available
Let self-indulgence teach you that where you think you lack
Is only the alone scared part of you soothing
herself through familiar neural pathways that can and will
Be directed to more helpful repetitive thoughts like

Who I am is always enough

DECEMBER 2

People do not want to be pushed, they want to be guided
Children especially when they lose what they thought would
support them

There is so much death
at all times, at various rates
for children suffering the loss
of elders, train yourself as a magician
to speak to them and allow them to feel, share and release
the dream that appears shattered
The family home is remarkably fragile and can break down

Do you not fear the mysteries that tell you that you will not
have Love again
Look Here for the Light
The egg breaks anew every Dawn I get to wake up and enjoy

12/3

Endure. We are out there changing lives for the better, starting
with ourselves.
The lesson is to trust myself to live and experience life

Author Note:
As I get close to finishing Volume One, Thank you so much
for taking the time to read and write books. Thank you so
much and I forgive you, Stephen King

DECEMBER 4

I have felt for a long time that I have been sitting on a rocket
It rumbles and cradles me
It supports my every vibration
Where is this sphere I sit on traveling?
Where is it taking me?
And then I realized the rocket was me

DECEMBER 5

Where did I go or could I have gone as a child to be supported?
What did or would my ideal have felt like?
Can I be that for my child now?

DECEMBER 6

Except the phase you are in now!
And have fun!

DECEMBER 7

Be patient. People really need my patience today. I can tell them how I feel, I can take care of myself and I can give them time. I can smile and have fun, I can look forward to the sun.

DECEMBER 8

What if I had never done anything with what I love. What do I love? I am going to make a list right now.

DECEMBER 9

I completely heal with my mother/primary caregiver and appreciate our differences.
I am not afraid to be who I am and nor is she

DECEMBER 10

"I am my job security."- Amanda Frances

DECEMBER 11

I run my finances and there is always plenty of money coming in! I get paid for my gifts, for my voice, for my authentic power. I am not pushy honey. I am guided by Integrity. There is no one above me, below me, just someone that wants to enjoy life within me.

DECEMBER 12

I have anxiety about anxiety
I have depression about depression
I am bigger than my negative thoughts
When Fear comes I duck and surrender
Whatever I look like, I choose to enjoy my Life.

DECEMBER 13

I am exquisite joy
I ask myself what that feels like in my body
And it's happiness
Thinking a friend is cute
Loving on a brother
Sending my enemy well wishes
Just this once
So I can set up and believe in a pattern
That reflects a reality
I CREATE from my Mind
My mind IS the answers and has the answer
To What I am afraid of

I am afraid of money in this moment
Will it run out? Will I go the ATM and be denied.
Does this reflect me?
Yes, and how I am feeling about my self and my ability to grow
It's okay to be me
It's okay to make money
I will not hurt anyone
Money does not hurt anyone
Money is fun!
I am fun!
I can make money
I can get paid for my gifts
I get paid for my gifts
I can stay away from guilty brain thoughts
that stir negative emotions up in me
Templeton teaching Wilbur
Skills of the rat brain
(reference to E.B. White's *Charlotte's Web*)

DECEMBER 14

There is female and a male within every organism, just looks
at plants
We take on female and male gender form to procreate
Make peace with your physical form

DECEMBER 15

Look forward, looking back hurt
A back scratch or a bottom smack,
I have met some folks with heartache
And I have met some folks with heartwarming news
As a human race, we are moving forward
I must move forward
If you are happy where you are,
it is by choice
It took me a long time to recognize this
There is a power working in us and through us that is way
beyond our understanding
Or is it?
You get to choose!

DECEMBER 16

To the part of me that cannot let go and be free, I am *Security*.
(I am the *Calm* part of you, _____.)

And from *Security*, I am introducing you to *Insecurity*, the
version of me that keeps showing up, keeps me craving, keeps
me doubting, depressed or fretting, hiding, isolated or trading
in over and over again for a better model.

I have so deeply rejected my *core-self* (from childhood) I change
what I look like, what I look at, desperately searching *for* and
simultaneously *hiding* and *rejecting* my *core-self*. I am a hard
nut to crack. I am the *false-self* in psychology, the chameleon,
addicted to the chemical rush of my own self-rejection.

I obsess on the subconscious core belief that me being valued *over or under/one up one down than* anyone will save me from how deeply I hate and reject what I *felt* as a child. My feelings store my cures. My guard is up, the fight is on but I continuously lose (my inner defeated loser) because I am too immature, undeveloped and subconsciously invisible to understand monogamous Love, for example, is a win/win. I trigger and fight with the *false-self* in others. I can only see my *false-self* if I choose to question myself.

I am traumatic attachment (abuse as to what I was or was not given: neglect, rejection, abandonment, the violence of silent treatment, I include lots of scenarios) Call me *Destroyer,* I am truly the part of me that self-destructs. Take a deep breathe, I am here to warn. I am as Real to you as is real for me. I treat you better when you treat me better. Get it? Good.

Just as far as I am emotionally aroused and physically connected to the inner experience I created *from within,* taking responsibility is taking the traumatic attachment that creates the *false-self* (the Narcissist for example) from the experience and seeing that humans are all fragile. Even as a childhood possibility, frees me to live an adult life free and clear of the guilt and insecurity the *false self* feeds on. My *false-self* rose to power to protect my *core-self* that was being so brainwashed by perceived rejection. No one rejected anyone, what if they were just busy and I was learning to defend myself.

What happened, the memory slide stored in the sensory filing cabinet of my amygdala, the storage house of my life curriculum responsible for my intake of sight, sounds, smells, sounds, tastes and touch, happened to teach me to pursue Joy.

I can accept and validate what happened and not make it my
identity
Where I am recreating the experience over and over in my life
is where I choose to look
I can trust how I feel about my trauma (whether it is from
what I did or did not get)
I am exactly where I am meant to be in my life.

DECEMBER 17

Even Hatred is reversed Love, you love possessing so much,
you hate.

DECEMBER 18

In my mind, I can push my shoulders back, hold my head up
high and glorify
That I showed up the best I could in the moment with the
knowledge and understanding
I had at the time, my coping mechanisms no longer lead me
to struggle
Love and intimacy are not as hard and scary as I have been
taught to believe
My partner is here already, my Queen or King is by my side
supporting me in my evolution

DECEMBER 19

Today is a beautiful day until so and so walks in and … (full of emotional pain and) so angry and…NOT today. Today I choose Peace. I choose to perpetuate Peace.

DECEMBER 20

I have been so insulted by matter of fact-o people because
I have undealt with emotional pain that fuels my self-doubt
And self-doubt cannot be trusted
Interacting with one another from self-doubt
You miss out on the lesson
What works for me, works for me
Life is fun!
If you take everything personally
You are constantly distracted from your purpose, don't just find joy, be joy

DECEMBER 21

Staying calm in a technical moment requires breathing slowly. I am rewiring my robot to breathe slowly and stay calm.

DECEMBER 22

I want my kids to be heirs, what about you?
I didn't grow up an heiress
I did not marry a Prince
But I became a Princess
A soon to be Queen
Finding and honoring a King

DECEMBER 23

Today is a great day to have a great day!
~ Dr. Iyanla Vanzant

DECEMBER 24

The upper most highest vibrations are within you
Whatever year it is, you are born to live out your life just as it is
If I chose or I was chosen, I will never know
I will be dead and gone
Or will I?
Allow these questions to guide your day
Especially when you are least strong
I felt all the fears you felt, nothing is new
It's already been done
It's already been lived out
The Grand Director just remains invisible

DECEMBER 25

I am so gullible and take witness to what I do and do not
Believe

DECEMBER 26

If we all believed in inherent good, how would the world be?
Would we be learning, pushing ourselves to know and
understand more
If I am dropped in to an already created world?
Where would I choose to go?
Right where I am?
Yes!

DECEMBER 27

Be absolutely certain with who you are
And you'll only question what really matters to you
You won't be caught up in office drama

Toxic people are distracting meaning they do things in
relationships
that are not normal and do not love and honor you
They are not honest, because they are not honest with
themselves
Their behavior is likely and not always about you
It's about them not feeling emotional pain (ie not feeling good
about themselves) that becomes toxic shame
If you get to a place where you love and honor yourself enough

you see toxic shame causes all sorts of disorders and addictions
All to avoid or get rid of toxic shame

I witness deep denial of oneself and one's character
They abuse themselves, they abuse others and do not apologize because
it's a threat to their *false-self* that they would have to admit is protecting by dishonoring
the *core-self/character* if they admitted responsibility

Toxic shame makes you feel like you can't help them
That's the one truth of toxic shame, you cannot help them
You cannot take on enough of their shame to heal them
They will keep coming back for more and confuse you
They must feel the emotional pain within themselves

DECEMBER 28

There was a time in my life when I was very afraid
It was five minutes ago
But I trust I have a profound purpose here
And believing anything otherwise is lazy

DECEMBER 29

Clarity of vision
Figure out what that means to you
We are built, I believe, to see black and white
In order to figure out how to get along
How are we doing?

How am I doing?

What getting along looks like is different for everyone
Define what it looks like to you
Getting along with everyone, not being their slave obviously
But living by self-defining principles
That exist anyway and are working in your life

1. Cause and Effect - my understanding of *C.& F.* is that my consciousness, whether I am aware of it or not, creates my reality. For example, what do I not like about my reality? a.) someone owes me a lot of money. If I do not want this experience, first, I deflect the pain of withholding from the other person and look where am I still withholding Love? And shift my thoughts. *Yes, money and love are connected.* Or if I am about to lose my job and everyone's been behaving like I am going to be let go but no one has told me yet. What do I do? I envision or write out what I want to happen, the more detail the better. I am expanding my relationship with God. I felt there was something more when I started to read about deliberately paying attention to thoughts via Consciousness. (Books I have read and mentioned are listed in *The Honorary Mentions.* My inner sarge was convinced and I was wildly curious. But I felt punished. So I started to *intentionally think, like right now* I am thinking about creating my Dynasty and what that feels like, "luxury and beyond" as Oprah says. Mother Theresa called it God. Whatever it is, go for it! Cause and effect is you! The more people we have in their purpose, the less distraction. And the less we are lead and abused by the mentally unstable, we can more and more live true to ourselves.

DECEMBER 30

Now I lay me down to sleep
The Lord, I pray my soul to keep
And if I die before I wake
The Lord, I pray, my Soul to take
Do not be taken over by your ambition
Ambition is a living and breathing thing
We are designed with various levels of ambition
I am so afraid of being world famous
But I know that's in the cards for me
Because the desire and vision is in my heart
If I do not live it out, I will be sick
How many of us are sick because we are not living out our vision
The desire within us - we are too attached to where we are born
who we are born to
focusing too much or not at all on childhood
is remaining a child in adulthood
And that is okay, we all have a place

The conundrum Loves is
To let go and truly, honestly be ourselves
Not at the sake of others
But *for* others - those in us, around and among us

DECEMBER 31

I have known for years now I would write political speeches
What talent are you hiding?

You can recalibrate your mindset
It requires Will and Grace
An ability to love and get along with yourself
Perhaps for the 1st time ever
Congratulations! Reach out. I want to hear about this experience for you
I know you are there, Your Mind is amazing, Your heart extraordinary
Your Mission already complete
A recollection of sea shells scattered along the shore of your soul
I see it all and I truly love you
Won't you adore me so I can give you Love

I feel so much better writing to you
Will you write back to me?
Paint me a picture?
Offer me an expression of you

Oh Lovelorn Lost!
Do not fret for too long
For then I cannot see you
I cannot find you
And love you more
Than you ever thought
Possible
I stand for you always Beloved

I am your token to any game
I am your Lover beside the flame
Your friend in the night
That dries your tears
and always, always happy you are here

See you in Volume Two? (;

HONORABLE BOOK MENTIONS:

"The Law of the Highest Potential," Robert Collier
"Intimacy Factor," Pia Mellody
"Get Over It!" Iyanla Vanzant
"A Gentle Path through the Twelve Steps," Patrick Carnes
"Boundaries for Dummies," Victoria Priya (Pre-Order)
"Goddesses Never Age," Christiane Northrup, M.D.
"Fifth Agreement," Don Miguel and Don Jose Ruiz
"Positive Mental Attitude," Napoleon Hill
"Happy Pocket of Money," David Cameron Gikandi
Wall Street Journal, Off Duty Section

Special Thanks to my coaches and mentors Darcy Iverson, Dr. Iyanla Vanzant, Rev/Coach Laura Rawlings/Deva Ji, Lali Ma and many others. Thank you so much.

Printed in the United States
by Baker & Taylor Publisher Services